Ripley Readers

Learning to read. Reading to learn!

LEVEL ONE Sounding It Out Preschool–Kindergarten
For kids who know their alphabet and are starting to sound out words.

learning sight words • beginning reading • sounding out words

LEVEL TWO Reading with Help Preschool–Grade 1
For kids who know sight words and are learning to sound out new words.

expanding vocabulary • building confidence • sounding out bigger words

LEVEL THREE Independent Reading Grades 1–3
For kids who are beginning to read on their own.

introducing paragraphs • challenging vocabulary • reading for comprehension

LEVEL FOUR Chapters Grades 2–4
For confident readers who enjoy a mixture of images and story.

reading for learning • more complex content • feeding curiosity

Ripley Readers Designed to help kids build their reading skills and confidence at any level, this program offers a variety of fun, entertaining, and unbelievable topics to interest even the most reluctant readers. With stories and information that will spark their curiosity, each book will motivate them to start and keep reading.

Vice President, Licensing & Publishing Amanda Joiner
Editorial Manager Carrie Bolin

Editor Jordie R. Orlando
Designer Luis Fuentes
Text Carrie Bolin
Reprographics Bob Prohaska

Chief Executive Officer Andy Edwards
Chief Commercial Officer Brett Clarke
Vice President, Global Licensing &
  Consumer Products Cassie Dombrowski
Vice President, Creative Dov Ribnick
Director, Brand & Athlete Marketing Ricky Melnik
Art Director & Graphic Designer Josh Geduld
Account Manager, Global Licensing &
  Consumer Products Andrew Hogan

Published by Ripley Publishing 2020

10 9 8 7 6 5 4 3 2 1

Copyright © 2020 Nitro Circus

ISBN: 978-1-60991-463-9

For more information regarding permission, contact:
VP Licensing & Publishing
Ripley Entertainment Inc.
7576 Kingspointe Parkway, Suite 188
Orlando, Florida 32819
Email: publishing@ripleys.com
www.ripleys.com/books

Manufactured in China in January 2020.

First Printing

Library of Congress Control Number: 2019942249

PUBLISHER'S NOTE
While every effort has been made to verify the accuracy of the entries in this book, the Publisher cannot be held responsible for any errors contained in the work. They would be glad to receive any information from readers.

WARNING
Some of the stunts and activities are undertaken by experts and should not be attempted by anyone without adequate training and supervision.

PHOTO CREDITS

Cover © Mark Watson/nitrocircus.com; **3** © Mark Watson/nitrocircus.com; **4-5** © Mark Watson - Nitro Circus/inciteimages.com; **6-7** © Andre Nordheim; **8-9** © Sam Neill; **10** © Christian Bertrand/Shutterstock.com; **12-13** © Nate Christenson; **14-15** © FrimuFilms/Shutterstock.com; **19** © Anatoliy Karlyuk/Shutterstock.com; **21** © Mark Watson - inciteimages.com; **22-23** © Mark Watson/nitrocircus.com; **24-25** © Nate Christenson; **26-27** © Mark Watson - inciteimages.com; **30-31** © Mark Watson - inciteimages.com

All other photos are courtesy of Nitro Circus. Every attempt has been made to acknowledge correctly and contact copyright holders, and we apologize in advance for any unintentional errors or omissions, which will be corrected in future editions.

NITRO CIRCUS
SCOOTER!

RIPLEY
PUBLISHING ®

a Jim Pattison Company

Nitro Circus is a group of men and women who perform stunts.

They go all over the world.

One of the sports they are best at is scooter.

This is a new sport.
Not many riders can do it.

Lots of scooter riders learn to ride a bike or skateboard first.

Riders use one foot
to push the scooter.

Scooter riders do not use
toy scooters to do tricks.

You can ride scooters on the street.

Some ride in parks.

One of the best scooter riders is Ryan Williams.

He is part of Nitro Circus.

21

He made a new trick
called the Silly Willy.

He spins and flips off
of a big ramp!

The best scooter riders go
to the Nitro World Games.

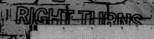

They try to do the best tricks that they can.

The riders use helmets
to stay safe.

They also use pads.

Stay safe and ride hard!

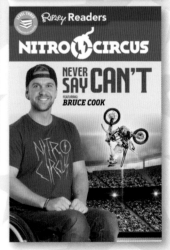